GW00976528

Copyright © 1995 Pickwick Group Ltd. All rights reserved.
Published by Pickwick Children's Entertainment, The Waterfront, Elstree, Hertfordshire, WD6 3BS.

**Q:** What fish only swims at night?

**A:** A starfish!

**Q:** What do bees use to make their hair look nice?

**A:** Honey combs!

**Q:** What makes a glow-worm glow?

**A:** It eats light meals!

**Q:** What game do cats play?

**A:** Trivial Purr-suit!

**Q:** Which animal on the ark was not in a pair?

**A:** The worms - they were in an apple instead!

**Q:** What animal has wooden legs?

**A:** A timber wolf!

**Q:** What is a cat's favourite breakfast snack?

**A:** Mice crispies!

**Q:** Why does a bear have a fur coat?

**A:** Because he'd look silly in a plastic raincoat!

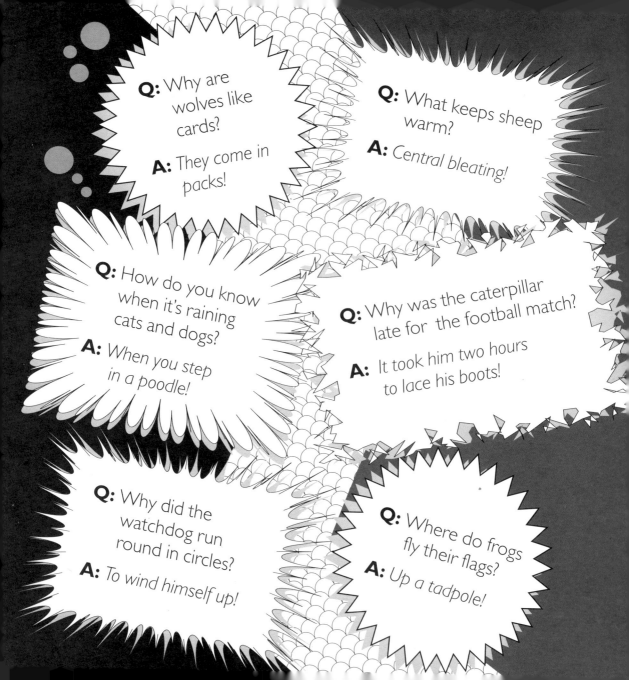

**Q:** Why do storks stand on one leg?

**A:** Because if they lifted two they'd fall over!

**Q:** What do you call three ducks in a crate?

**A:** A box of quackers!

**Q:** What do you call a puma from Poland?

**A:** A pole-cat!

**Q:** Why did the bull have his eyes closed?

**A:** Because he was bull-dozin!

**Q:** What does a cat rest his head on?

**A:** A caterpillar!

**Q:** What's the best advice to give a worm?

**A:** Sleep late!

**Q:** What is black, white and red?

**A:** A polar bear with sunburn and dirty paws!

**Q:** Where do monkeys put their babies?

**A:** *In apri-cots!*

**Q:** What has six legs and always does its homework?

**A:** *A fly swat!*

**Q:** What is the best way to hunt bear?

**A:** *With no clothes on!*

**Q:** What's white, furry and smells of peppermint?

**A:** *A polo bear!*

**Q:** Where do hamsters go on holiday?

**A:** *Hamsterdam!*

**Q:** Why didn't the woodworm eat the sofa and armchair?

**A:** *Because he didn't like to eat suites between meals!*

**Q:** What was the tortoise doing on the M1?

**A:** *About five metres an hour!*

**Q:** What goes thud, squelch, thud, squelch?

**A:** An elephant with one wet shoe!

**Q:** Why did the zebra wear a spotty pair of pyjamas?

**A:** His striped ones were in the wash!

**Q:** Why do rhino's ha[ve] wrinkled feet?

**A:** Because their shoelaces are too tight!